'Lines For You'

This book is dedicated to my
dearest mum and family in
Istanbul, Turkey

If you are reading this,
remember, these lines are for
you - wherever you are, you are
not alone.
I feel you, I really do.
You first need to believe in
yourself - to make it happen.
Be different, be you.
Speak your words.
Tell your stories.
Dream higher, love bigger.
This is how you grow and glow.

Love,
Sonay x

LINES FOR YOU

SONAY

New Generation Publishing

You made me believe in fairy
tales and it was lit.

Your loved ones may leave but
their memories will stick to your
soul forever.
Love is powerful and eternal.

The one who left did not return,
the one who stayed did not
forget.

Magic is yet to come.

Summer sunsets,
Night skies,

Long conversations,
Old letters and the vague
memory of you.

You are haunting me.

We were dancing under the ray
of fireworks till the end of time.
Then you smiled.

Once upon a time
or
at a time once happened?

I will let you decide.

If someone refuses to accept
your love and respect, despite
you trying your best – believe
me, someday they would regret
losing you.

Between you and me,
there are planets
--- and ---
galaxies.

Now or never.
Not taking the risk is the biggest
risk, you would regret it forever.

We said goodbye forever the
last time we saw each other but
you were right, we were already
heartbroken.

Opening my heart left a blood
stain.

A part of me will always be with
you and miss you.

You and your flaws are my
favourite lies.

I never forgot the first and last
day we said goodbye.

Time does not make it easier
but it helps me adjust to the
idea of you being a 'memory'
now.

It is all about you.
It has always been you.

You bloom every day within the
garden of secret angels in my
dreams.

Never let anyone make you feel
like an option, know your worth.

Whatever you do - put your
heart, mind and spark into it.
You eventually get what you
deserve.
This is 'passion'.

Find your passion which sets
your soul on fire.

I am unpredictable,
but
so are you.

You are a star, flung out of
space.
Composed of lights, colours and
a little bit of magic.

Finding out the truth hit me hard after many years. After a long period of healing – I now truly believe that everything happens for a reason, every person has a role in our lives.

There is a plan written in the stars.

Yellow was my favourite colour.
I loved everything in yellow.
I found yellow in every bit of
spark

-      in every inch of you.

Are you thinking too much?
Is it too much to handle?
Are you drowning under the
rain?

You are an overthinker.
You are not alone.

Self-sufficiency is the key to
success.
Never lose your passion.
Have no limits.
Shine bright.
Feel magic.
Be magical.

Remember – whoever you are,
you are very special.

They would avoid you if they
know that they did you wrong
or treated you badly.

This is an absolute fact.

It stings when something
beautiful reminds me of you
and your colours.

I wish I could paint you black,
but black would still look so
good on you.

Colour me in and watch me fly
— to brighten your sky.

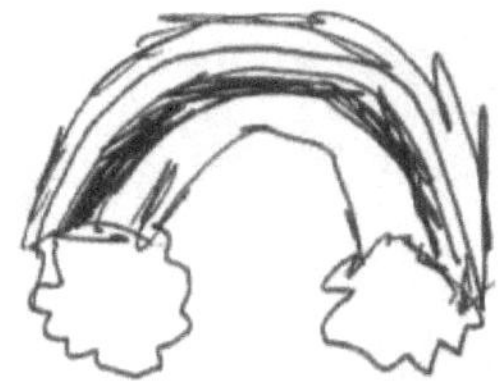

Some are blessings, some are
lessons. Every person crossing
your path serves a purpose.
They help you to heal and grow,
for you to become a better
version of yourself.

If someone loves you
unconditionally, they would
always love you despite your
flaws.

This is pure love, keep those
ones close.

-        closer than the sun.

I have too many unsent letters,
Unsaid words and unwritten
thoughts.

If you read them all,
you would be in tears.

Did you ever think of me as
much as I did think of you?

Did we think of each other
simultaneously?

Did you ever feel like crying
when a song reminded you of
me?

There is no growth in replaying
old conversations or going back
to past memories.

Move on.

It is okay to miss them but
remember the reason why they
are not in your life anymore.

Remember, how you felt when
they broke you and how they let
you down.

Forgive them, let it go.

The moon and the stars.
Both told me stories at night.
I had so much to write but no
one would know how much I
carried in my heart.
I am afraid I would lose you
twice if you ever knew what was
in my mind.

I read every line, keeping your
words to myself.

Word by word – not to forget
you, not to let you go, until your
'memory' faded away and left a
scar.

Every friendship has an expiry
date.
You will lose friends.
Sooner or later, you will.

You would know their true
colours when they are gone.

No matter how genuine you are,
at the end of the day, you end
up treating people like how they
treated you.

Can you look at me like
somebody new?

At least try.

I never expected people to
understand me because, sadly,
most of them would never know
what unconditional love is.

If they walk away, you should let
them go. You just need to face
the fact that their role in your
life has come to an end.

Sad but true.

Everyone has a way of saying
goodbye on their terms.

I write letters.
What about you?

He promised her forever.
He said 'forever smells like you'.
Then hugged her in his big arms.

She said 'do not break my
he(art)'.

For the last time, she turned
around and did not look back
again.

There was so much left unsaid.
Unspoken words.
London felt her tears.

Dear old me,

Thank you for believing in me,
despite the worst odds and
rejection, you did it.

You are now living your dream.

Indifference hurts more than
rejection.

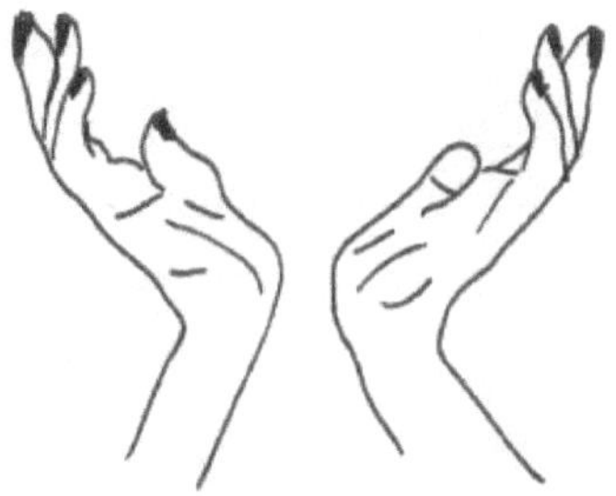

The way how people leave your
life would tell you so much
about them and what you did
not already know.

Goodbye forever until next
time.

Please do not ever forget me.

Pinky promise?

Sonay Beyatli is a medical
doctor, an academic respiratory
specialist registrar working in
London, the United Kingdom.
Her hobbies are writing poetry,
making music – creating all
forms of art.